STAR WARS®

JUMBO COLORING AND ACTIVITY BOOK

bendon
The BENDON name, logo, and Tear and Share are trademarks of Bendon, Inc., Ashland, OH 44805.

CONSTABLE
ZUVIO

MILLENNIUM FALCON

FIRST ORDER STAR DESTROYER

SARCO

BB-8
ASTROMECH
DROID

FINN

STAR WARS

RESISTANCE WORD SEARCH

X	A	J	Q	K	G	R	N	P	H	O	I	D
S	W	M	I	L	L	E	N	N	I	U	M	F
A	T	I	P	Q	U	Y	I	U	O	C	H	A
S	B	A	N	G	F	K	F	V	T	H	A	L
T	C	5	R	G	M	N	E	O	N	E	N	C
R	D	R	V	F	Q	O	I	J	N	W	S	O
O	U	L	S	R	I	P	N	O	Z	B	O	N
M	V	W	V	2	U	G	R	Y	7	A	L	A
E	D	M	T	D	E	E	H	B	A	C	O	Z
C	R	K	L	2	M	E	F	T	D	C	L	Y
H	O	L	C	A	C	3	P	O	E	A	E	W
S	I	R	D	R	K	M	S	T	I	R	I	J
E	D	E	S	P	E	E	D	E	R	2	A	B
C	O	G	E	C	N	A	T	S	I	S	E	R
P	F	H	R	E	P	O	O	R	T	B	B	8

RESISTANCE TROOPER
REY, FINN
SPEEDER
LUKE, LEIA
HAN SOLO
BB-8
C-3PO
R2-D2
MILLENNIUM FALCON
CHEWBACCA
X-WING STARFIGHTER
POE DAMERON
ASTROMECH
DROID

STAR WARS

FIND THE DIFFERENCE

Circle the drawing of Rey that is different.

ANSWER: C

REY

REY'S SPEEDER

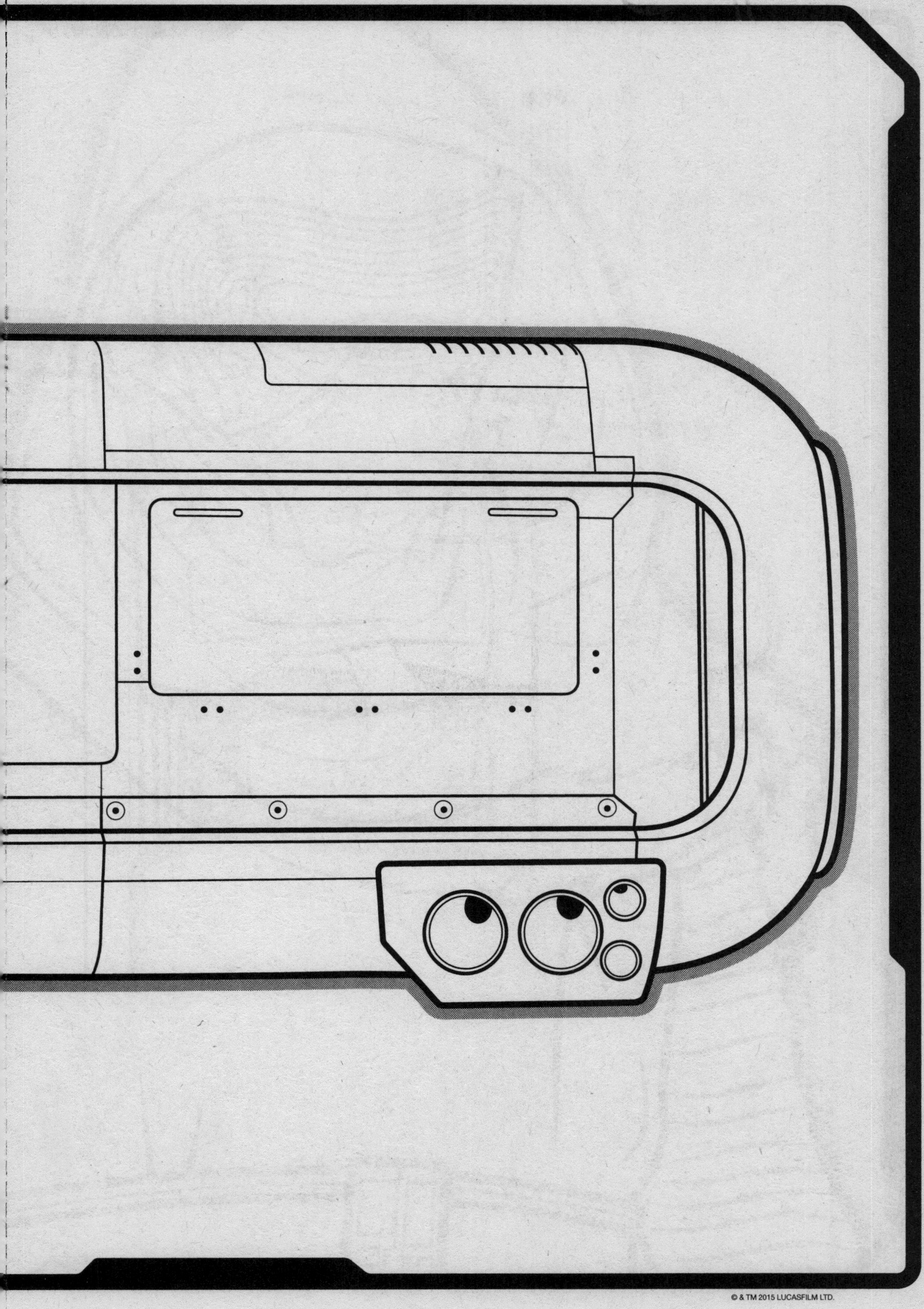

KYLO REN

CAPTAIN PHASMA

STAR WARS

FIND THE DIFFERENCE

Circle the drawing of Kylo Ren that is different.

ANSWER: D

STAR WARS

Make different words from the letters in

CAPTAIN PHASMA

POSSIBLE ANSWERS: SAP, PAN, CAN, TAN, STAIN, PAIN, RAT, MAT, MIT

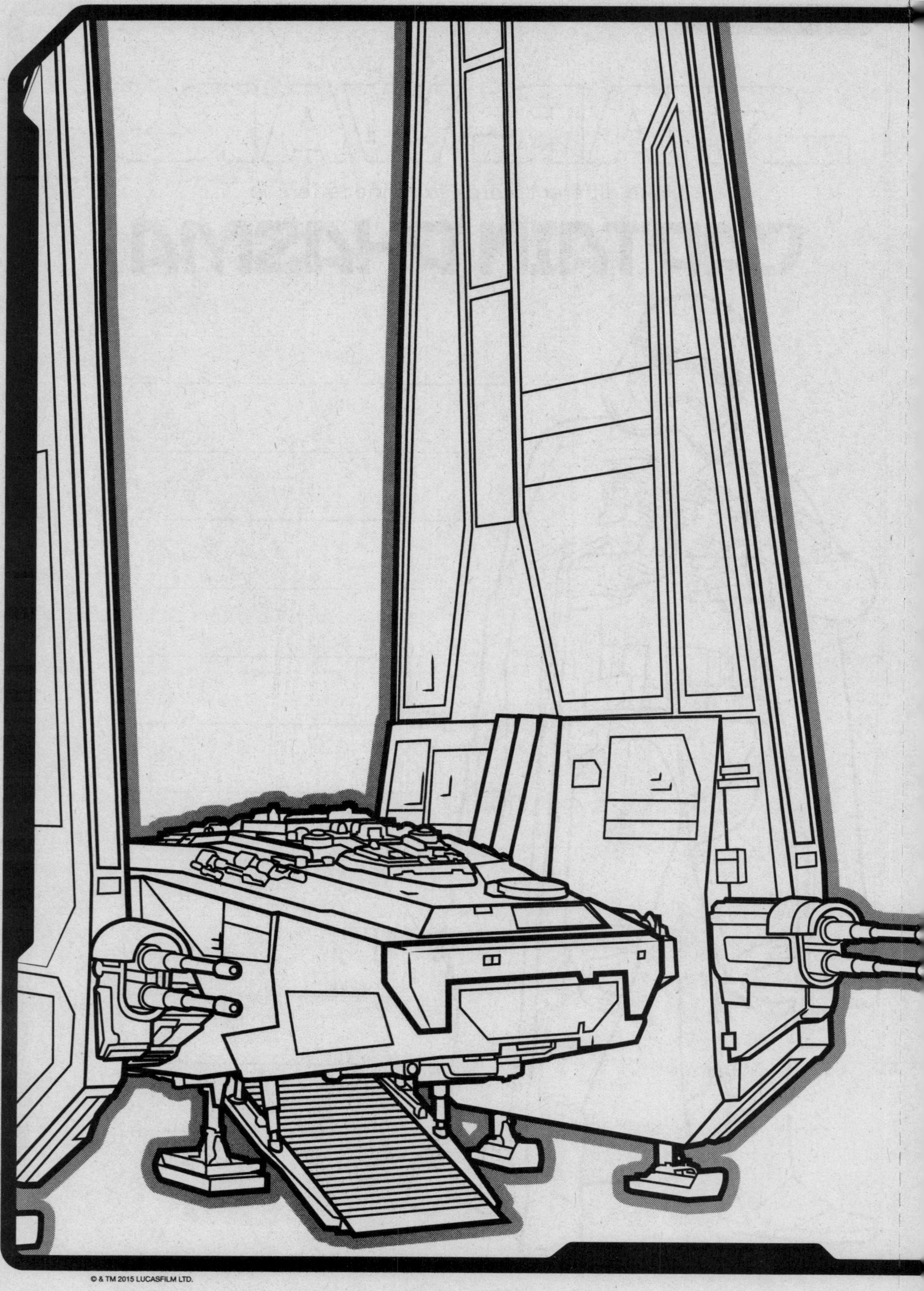

KYLO REN'S COMMAND SHUTTLE

GUAVIAN DEATH GANG

PZ-4CO

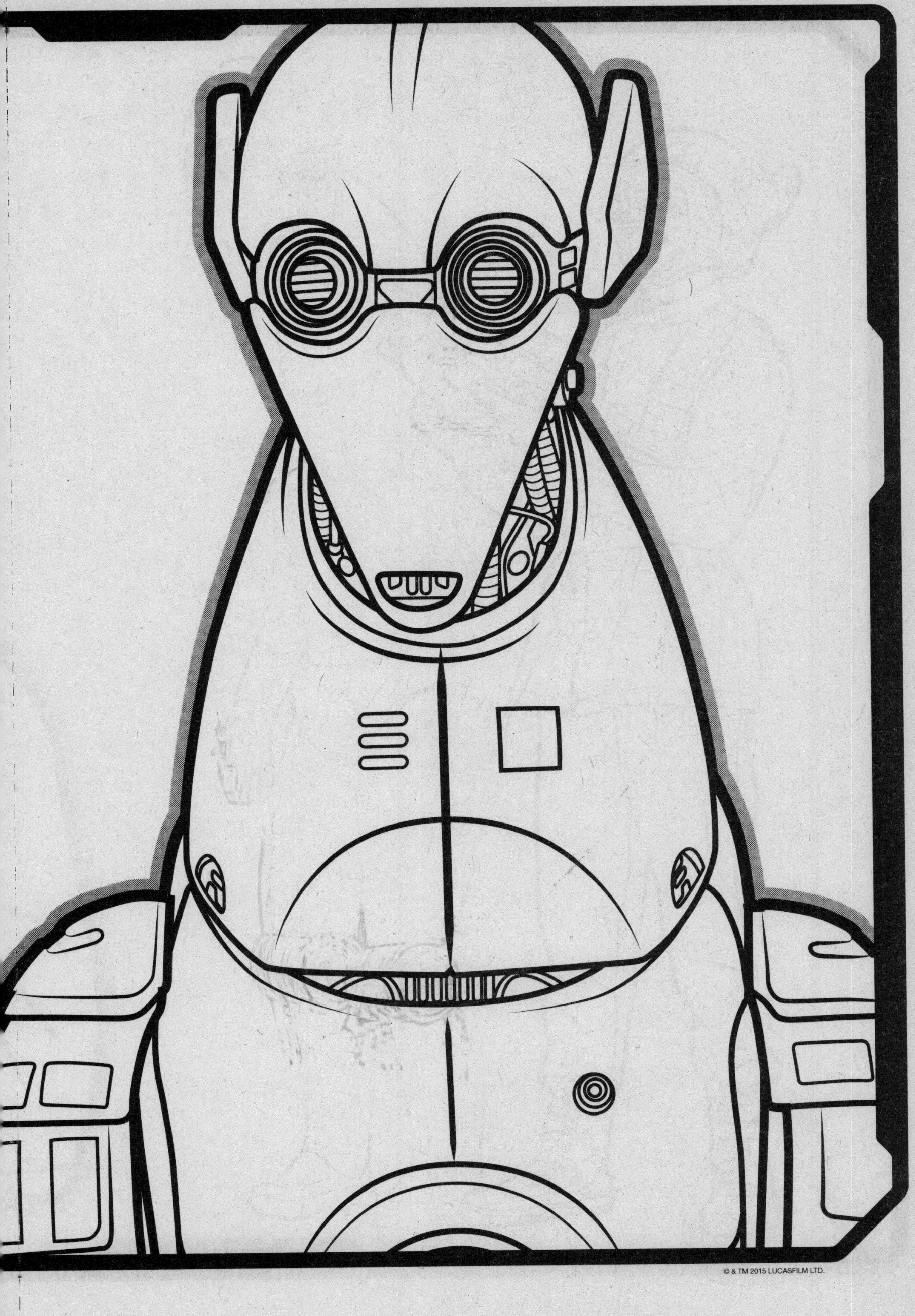

RESISTANCE TROOPER

TEEDO

© & TM 2015 LUCASFILM LTD.

CHEWBACCA

R2-D2

C-3PO

POE DAMERON

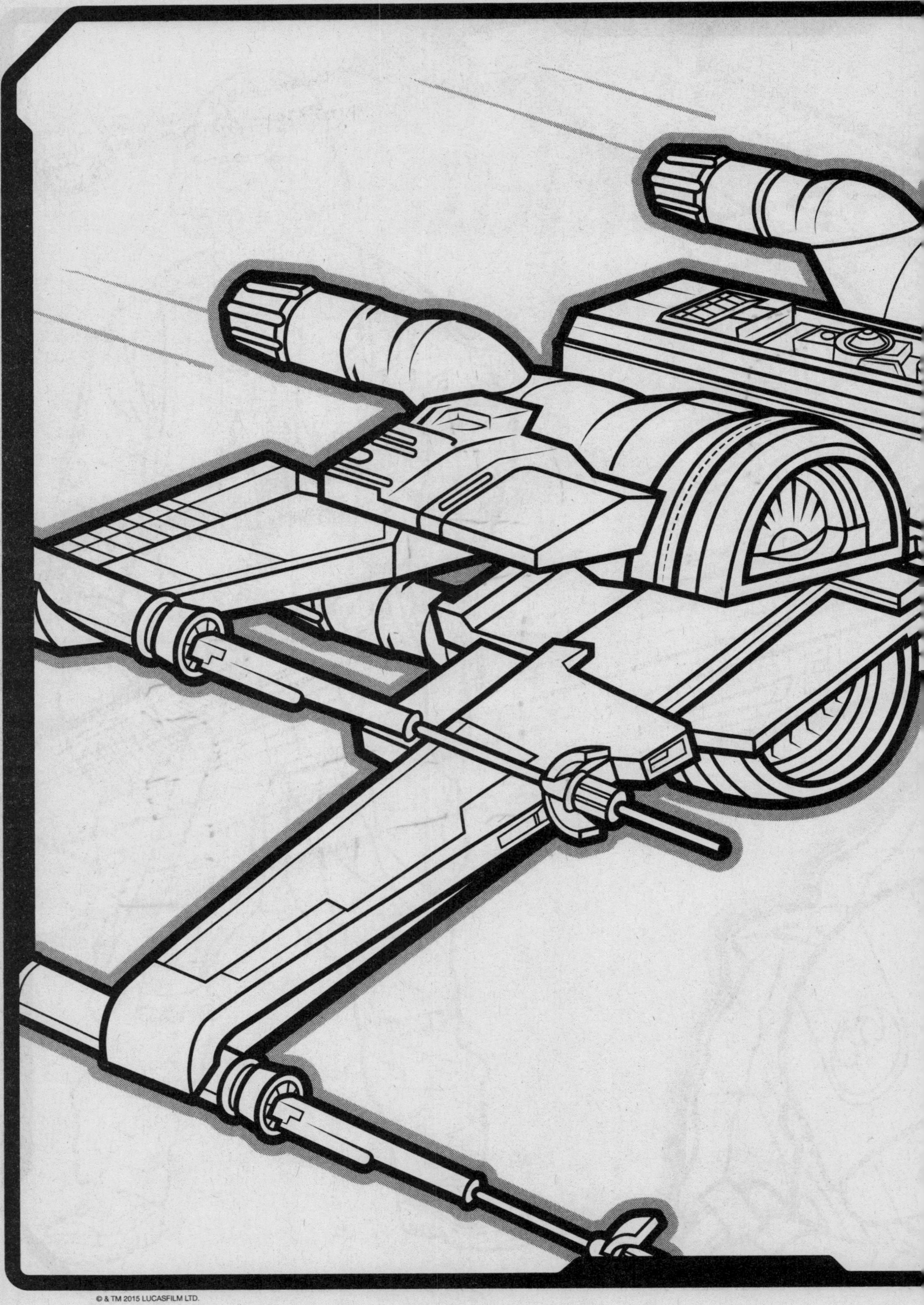

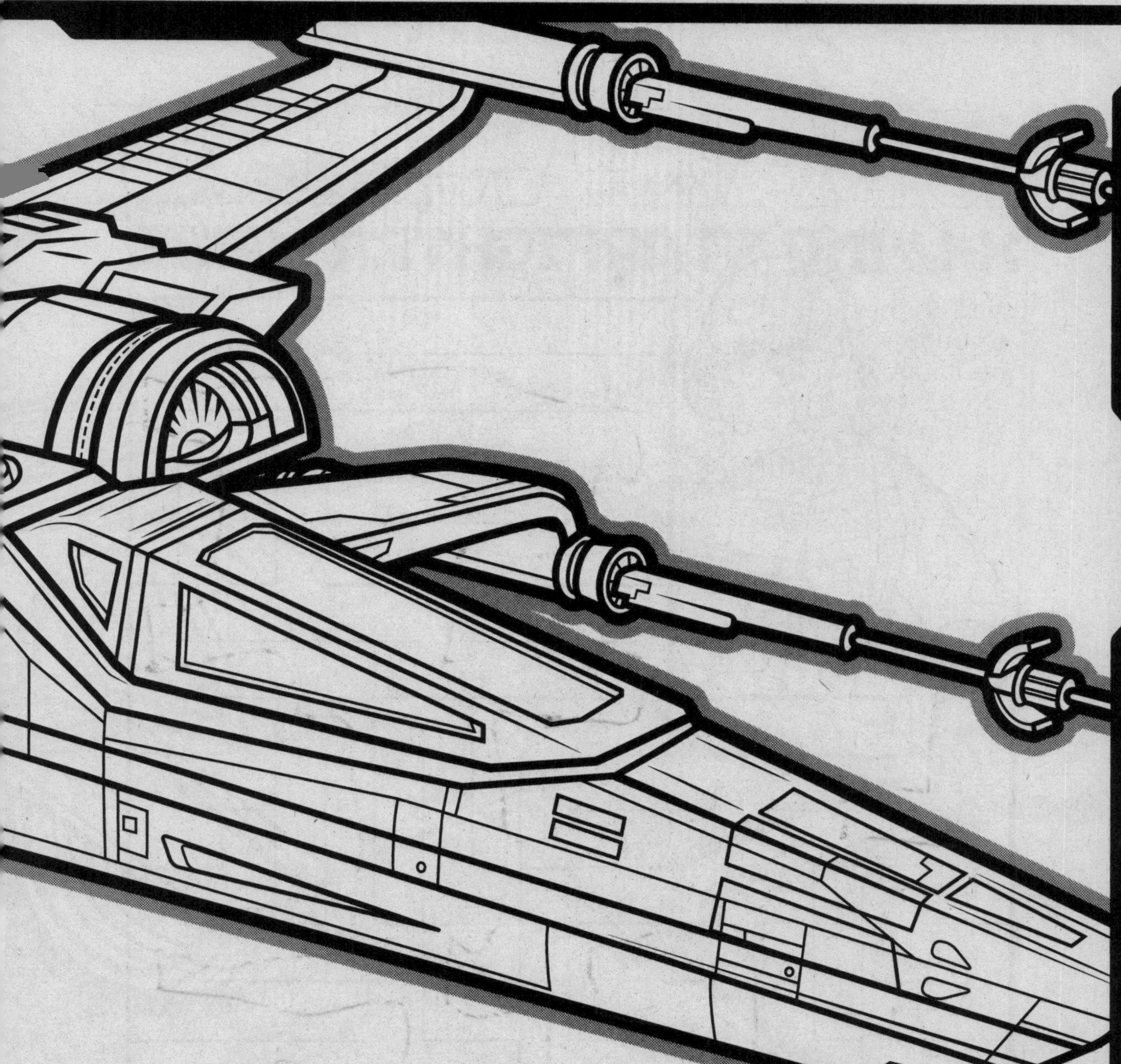

T-70 X-WING STARFIGHTER

STAR WARS

X-WING STARFIGHTER MAZE

Lead Poe through the maze to his fighter!

STAR WARS

WHICH PATH TO FOLLOW?

Which path leads Finn and BB-8 to Rey and her speeder?

ANSWER: B

LUGGABEAST

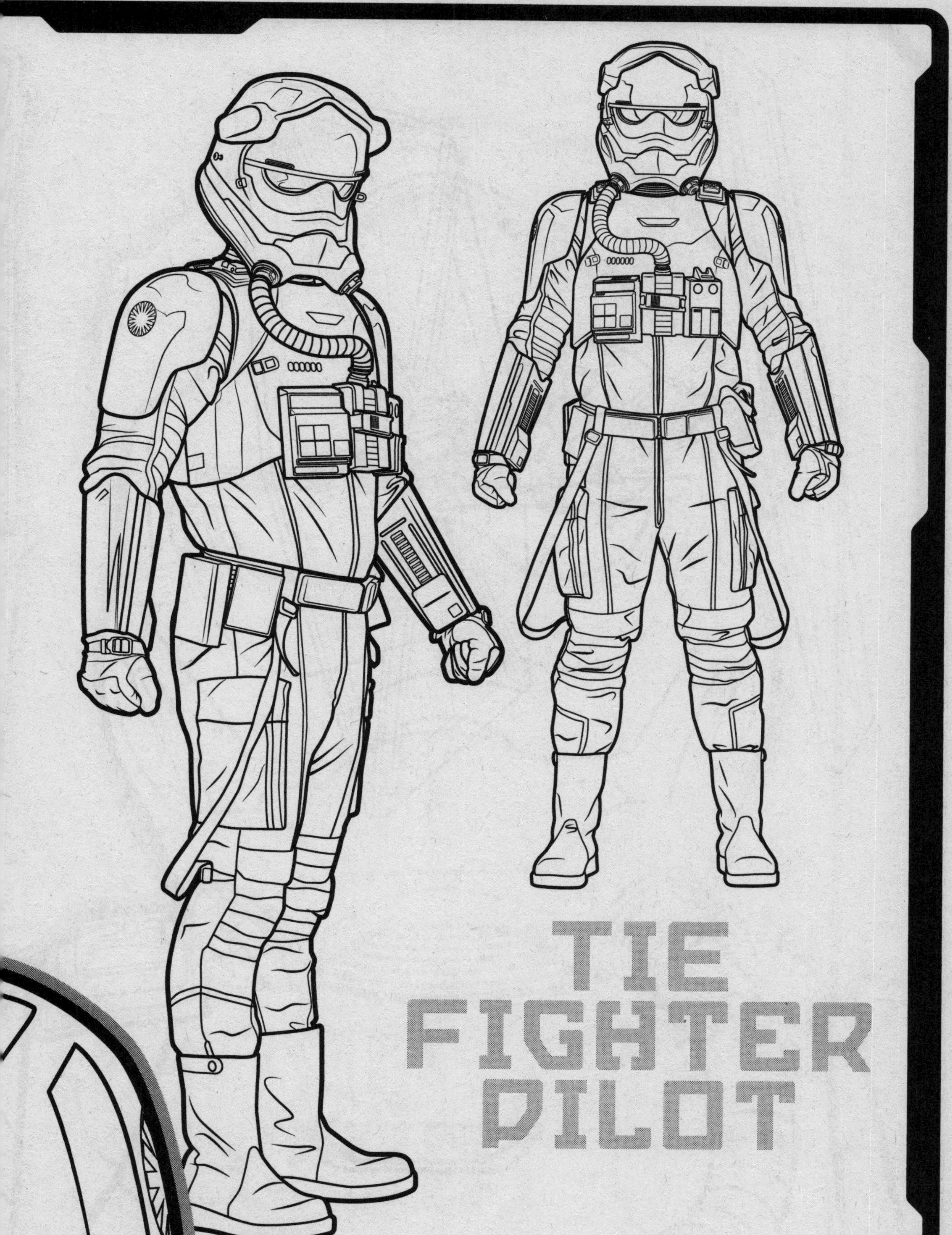

TIE FIGHTER PILOT

FIRST ORDER TIE FIGHTERS

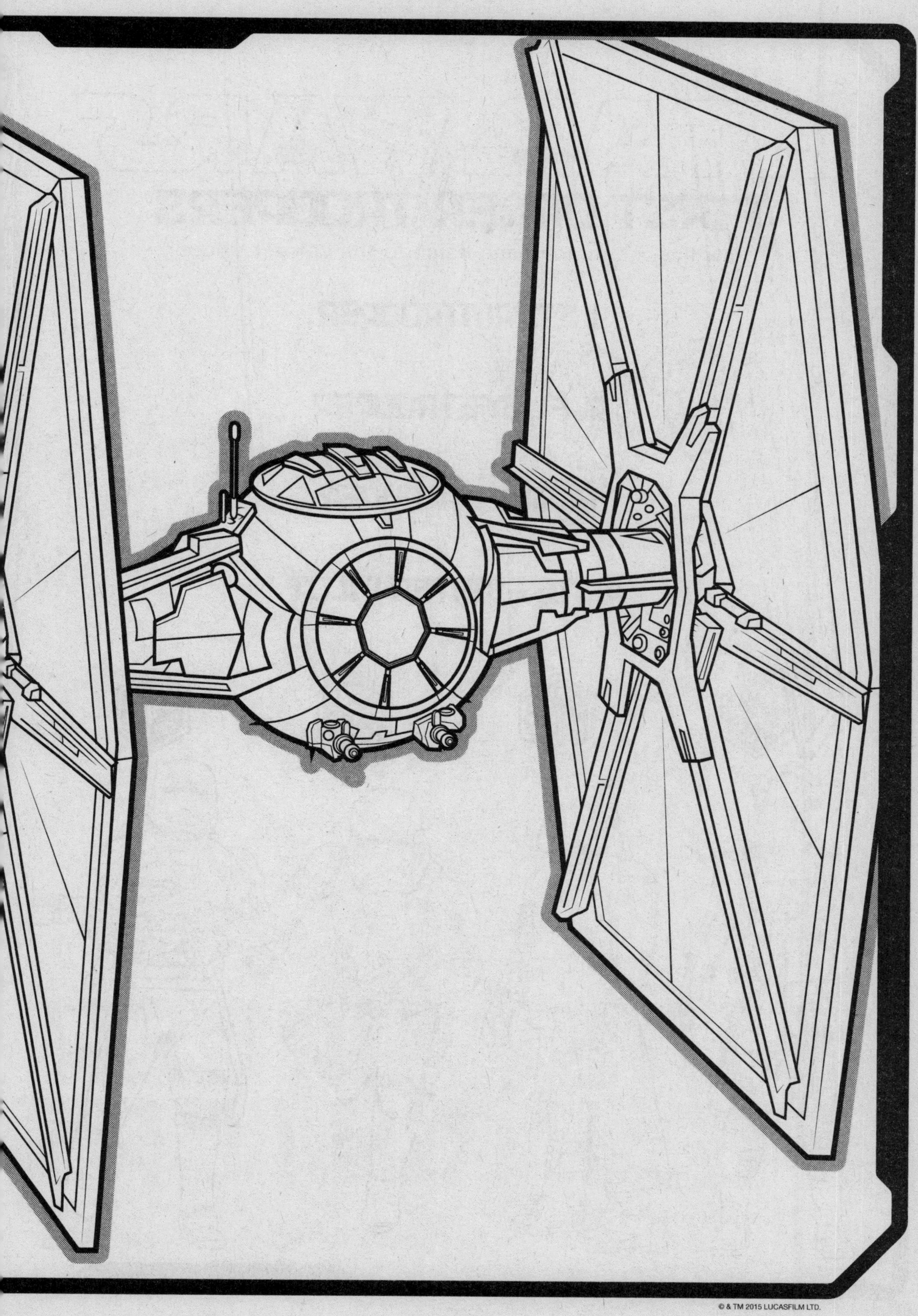

STAR WARS

FIRST ORDER TROOPERS

Draw lines to match each name to the correct trooper.

1. STORMTROOPER

2. FLAMETROOPER

3. SNOWTROOPER

4. TIE FIGHTER PILOT

ANSWERS: 1–C, 2–D, 3–B, 4–A

STAR WARS

TIE FIGHTER MAZE

Lead the TIE fighter pilot through the maze to his fighter!

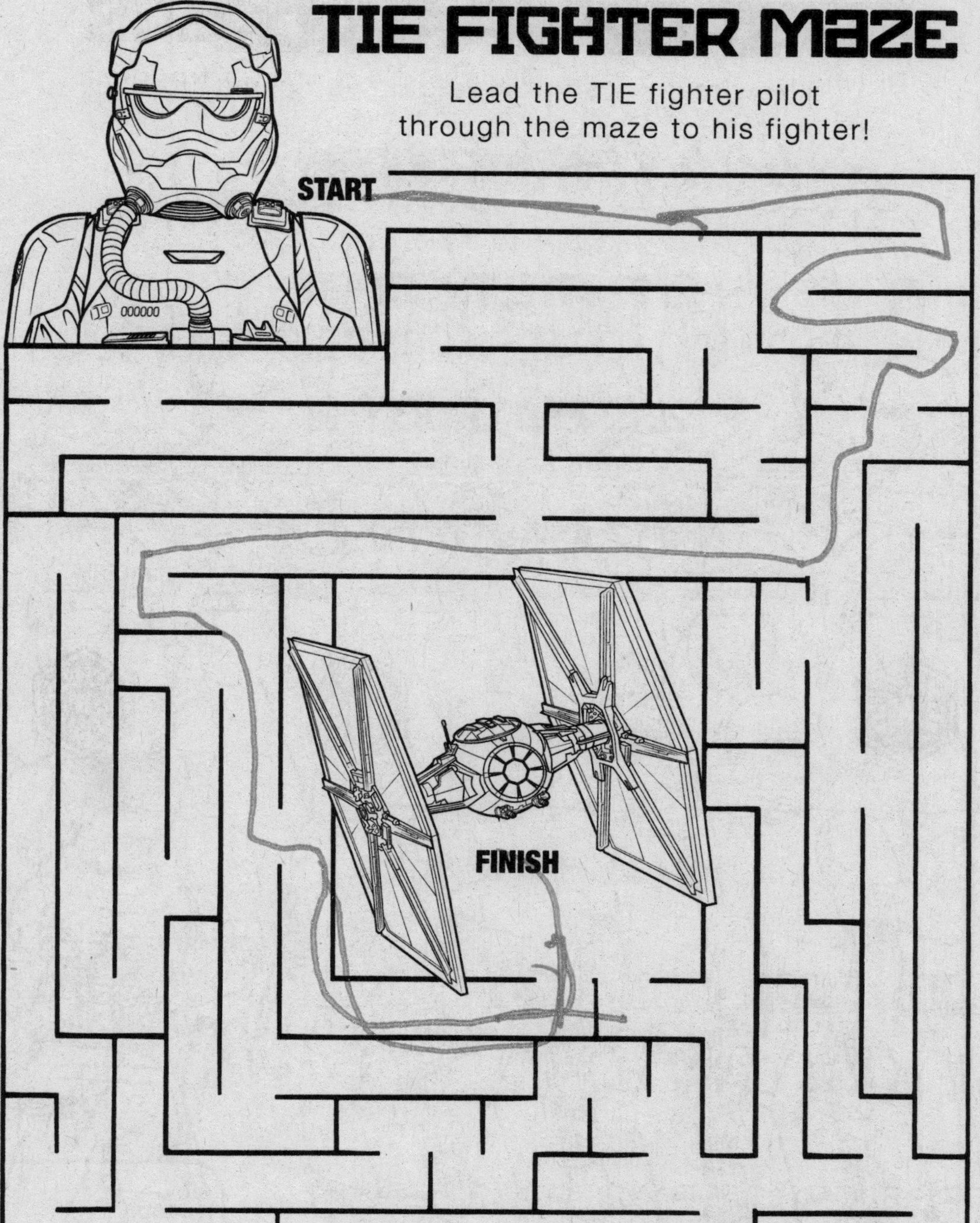

STAR WARS

SHOW OF FORCE!

How many stormtroopers do you count?

YOUR ANSWER

ANSWER: 21

STAR WARS

FIRST ORDER WORD SEARCH

C	D	S	B	L	A	S	T	E	R	F	C	F
S	A	E	T	R	I	F	L	E	N	I	D	L
T	U	P	S	A	B	P	O	W	E	R	I	A
O	T	P	T	T	R	A	L	M	O	S	J	M
R	I	A	R	A	R	P	W	Y	Z	T	K	E
M	E	Q	D	E	I	O	B	R	Q	O	S	T
T	F	R	A	K	M	N	Y	C	T	R	P	R
R	I	S	R	Y	F	E	P	E	U	D	O	O
O	G	D	K	L	T	O	L	H	R	E	N	O
O	H	E	S	O	U	G	R	E	A	R	M	P
P	T	F	I	R	A	V	Y	C	A	S	L	E
E	E	H	D	E	W	Z	J	K	E	D	M	R
R	R	G	E	N	H	I	S	N	O	K	E	A
E	F	S	N	O	W	T	R	O	O	P	E	R
R	E	Y	O	R	T	S	E	D	R	A	T	S

STORMTROOPER
SNOWTROOPER
FLAMETROOPER
TIE FIGHTER
STAR DESTROYER

FIRST ORDER
SUPREME LEADER
CAPTAIN PHASMA
KYLO REN
POWER

DARK SIDE
FORCE
BLASTER
RIFLE

FIRST ORDER SNOWTROOPER

FLAMETROOPER

FIRST ORDER RIOT CONTROL TROOPER